After the
DINOSAURS
The Story of Prehistoric Mammals and Man

After the DINOSAURS
The Story of Prehistoric Mammals and Man

By James C. Shooter
Illustrated by Peter Barrett

A GOLDEN BOOK · NEW YORK
Western Publishing Company, Inc.
Racine, Wisconsin 53404

Table of Contents

Glyptodon

Pantolambda

INTRODUCTION

How did the world begin? How did it become what it is today? For ages people have asked these questions and others like them. During the last few thousand years people have kept written records of what happened. But what about still earlier times? What happened then?

No one knows for certain what took place long ago, before records were kept. Those times are called **prehistoric**, which means "before history." In order to figure out what happened in prehistoric times, people study **fossils**, which are the remains of old bones, and other kinds of evidence. From these clues they try to guess what kinds of creatures used to live in the world, and what the world was like back then.

Many of the guesses, or **theories**, that people have made about the prehistoric world are very probably true. Many more, however, are less certain, and some are still just hunches. Sometimes even the theories that seem most certain must be changed when new evidence is discovered.

This book is based upon the theories that are the most certain or most widely accepted now.

Someday new discoveries may change people's minds about the theories presented here. The only thing that is for sure, it seems, is that people will never stop asking questions about Earth's prehistoric past.

Jellyfish

Sea pens

Flatworm

Worms

Very early life-forms

Where There Is Hope . . . There Is Life!

The first living thing was a simple tiny creature, drifting in the sea over four billion years ago. Eventually it reproduced by dividing itself in two. And that was the start of something big. All living things descended from that first creature.

The key to the future of life was in the process by which the first creature divided. The way it happened showed that it was possible for living things to change from generation to generation. This sort of change is called **evolution**.

Slowly more and more living things populated the seas. As time passed, some changed, or evolved, into new and different kinds of living things.

Together, all the external factors that affect a living thing are called its **environment**. An environment is more than just a place where something lives. It includes the other living things present, because living things often affect each other. Some prey upon others. Some compete with others for food, territory, or mates. Some are helpful to others. Some affect each other indirectly by causing changes in each other's surroundings. Natural forces like volcanoes and earthquakes can cause changes in surroundings, too.

Whether a particular kind of living thing thrives or not depends upon how well it interacts with its environment, and sometimes how well it copes with changes in its environment. In the past, some kinds of living things interacted with their environments very successfully and became very abundant for a while.

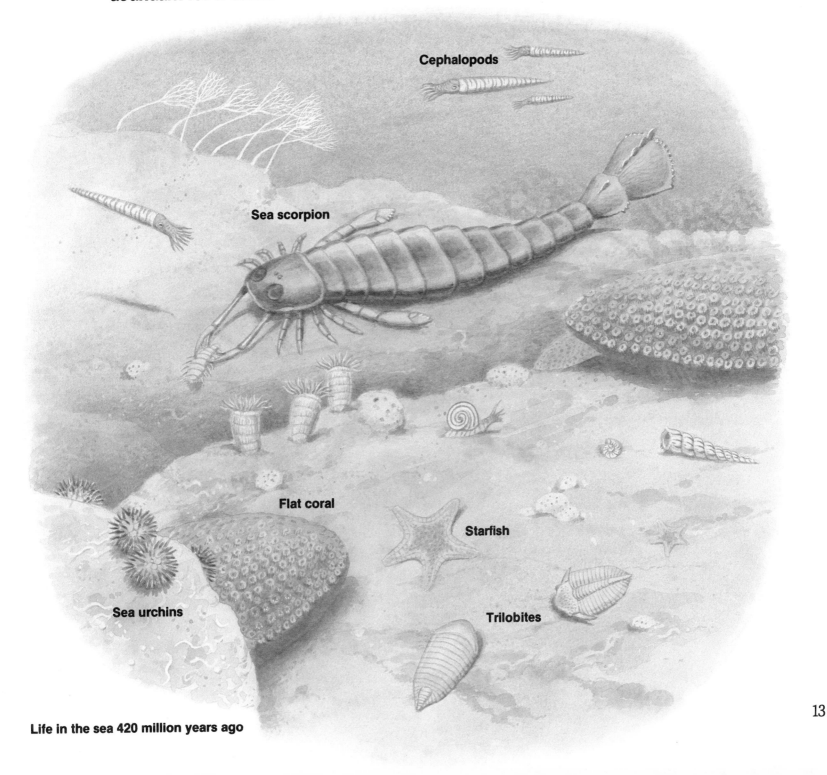

Cephalopods

Sea scorpion

Flat coral

Starfish

Sea urchins

Trilobites

Life in the sea 420 million years ago

13

The first amphibian was called Ichthyostega.

What about the less successful ones? Some simply died out. Some scraped by. Some found new places to live. Usually those were places where the environment was different. Life-forms that braved harsh conditions in new places sometimes evolved and adapted to their new homes over time.

It is also probably true that sometimes, as living things evolved within one environment, by chance they would develop new abilities that allowed them to spread into new environments.

For these reasons living things seem to enter every place possible. Wherever there is any hope of survival, it seems there is life, struggling, fighting, trying.

It was only a matter of time until some living things left the sea and made their way onto dry land.

Plants and insects came first. Then, 350 million years ago, **amphibians** began crawling ashore. Amphibians are creatures that spend part of their lives in water and part on land.

Dimetrodon

Petrolacosaurus

16

Conquerors of the New World

When the first life-forms left the sea to live on land, the stage was set for drama. In the world beyond the waters, amphibians faced many difficulties. Over many millions of years some of them evolved and adapted. Eventually two new types of creatures evolved from amphibian ancestors, and a 200-million-year struggle for mastery over Earth began.

One group of new creatures, the **cotylosaurs**, were **reptiles**. Reptiles are scaly-skinned creatures that lay eggs on dry land.

The other type were the **pelycosaurs**, the earliest forerunners of **mammals**. Mammals are creatures with hair or fur that give birth to live babies instead of laying eggs, and that nurse their young.

Reptilelike cotylosaurs were sluggish when the weather was cool. The mammal-like pelycosaurs had better body-temperature controls and were better able to handle changes in the weather—a big advantage.

The cotylosaurs, which lived close to the water and ate plants and insects, were usually no match for their savage meat-eating enemies—especially the razor-toothed 12-foot monster **Dimetrodon**, king of the pelycosaurs.

The Reptiles Strike Back

After ruling Earth for tens of millions of years, the mammal-like pelycosaurs were gradually replaced by their descendants, the **therapsids**. The therapsids were even more like modern mammals than the pelycosaurs. Most of them were quick, deadly hunters, but some were plant-eaters. Even the plant-eaters were big, strong, and dangerous, though.

The therapsids dominated the world even more completely than their predecessors had.

But things were changing. One group of reptiles was evolving slowly from insect-eaters into fish-eaters, hunters, and scavengers. Their hind legs and tails grew more powerful, making them better swimmers and, at the same time, faster runners.

These bigger, faster, more dangerous reptiles were called **thecodonts**. Most of the time they stayed along the rivers and beaches like the reptiles before them. The therapsids remained the dominant land animals.

But then, because of shifting in Earth's crust, the waters of the oceans began to withdraw, the land became drier, and some rivers disappeared.

At the same time the climate was slowly turning warmer, which was better for the reptiles. Reptiles are more active in hot weather.

Lystrosaurus

As the world gradually changed around them, many thecodonts evolved even further, into true **dinosaurs**, which were bigger and fiercer still. Around 200 million years ago many varieties of these new animals evolved very quickly.

Then, with amazing suddenness, the dinosaurs left the mud-clogged rivers and barren beaches and invaded the mighty therapsids' own grounds, often attacking and battling the therapsids head-to-head. It must have been like a war.

In only a few million years the therapsids were almost entirely destroyed, and the dinosaurs were Earth's new kings.

Coelophysis

Kannemeyeria

Anchisaurus

The Once and Future Kings

Only the smallest, most ratlike therapsids survived the mass slaughter carried out by the dinosaurs, and even these therapsids died out soon afterward.

However, shortly before the sudden end of the therapsids' rule, the first mammal had evolved from therapsid predecessors. It was a shrewlike creature called **Morganucodon**. Morganucodon survived, and so did several other small mammals that had evolved during the last days of the therapsids.

For the most part these mammals hid under rocks, in tree stumps, and in holes during the day, and dared to creep out and search for food only at night.

What else could they do? Out in the open, in broad daylight, how could any rodent-sized mammal put up a fight against six tons of hungry, charging Allosaurus?

20

Melanosaurus

Rhamphorhynchus

Triceratops

Catastrophe!

Sixty-five million years ago the dinosaurs' reign over Earth came to a sudden end. All of the dinosaurs, and many other living things as well, died out completely in a very short period of time.

No one is certain how it happened, or what caused it, but more and more evidence points to a **cosmic catastrophe**.

The beginning of the end for the dinosaurs may have been a typical spring day. Ceratopsians fed peacefully on thick-stemmed plants. In the distance, a herd of duck-billed hadrosaurs honked and hooted to each other as they loped along toward the river. And, as always, the mighty meat-eating Tyrannosaurus rex lurked nearby among the trees.

Anatosaurus

Suddenly a light filled the sky. An object 10 miles across appeared above. It was a **comet** falling like a monstrous hammer from space. There was no time to blink at its brilliance.

It hit. The force of the impact was equivalent to 20 billion atomic bombs.

It shook the entire planet. Everything in a vast area around the impact point was instantly wiped out. A huge fireball surged skyward. A wave of searing heat scorched much of the globe. Firestorms swirled through the atmosphere, burning whole forests in a flash. Death was everywhere.

But those were only the first effects. . . .

The Aftermath

The death toll was awesome. Most larger animals, like dinosaurs and other giant reptiles, probably died immediately.

But many creatures survived. Some lizards, snakes, and mammals were underground or under cover. Some crocodiles and turtles were also protected. A number of birds and mammals that lived in cold, sheltered mountainous regions survived. The hardiest things that lived in the sea, and those that lived in deep water, survived, and so did the insects.

The world the survivors faced was a bleak one, however. Dust darkened the sky for months. Rain fell almost constantly, carrying down chemicals created by the blast. Lakes, rivers, and even parts of the ocean became poisoned. In many places snow fell instead of rain, because dust and clouds blocked the sunlight, making the climate cooler. The effect lasted for years. In some places the years right after the impact must have seemed like one long winter.

Any dinosaurs that may have survived the first awful moments of the catastrophe probably died soon afterward.

Somehow many of the mammals struggled through by eating insects, decaying plants, and the rotting remains of dead animals.

Eventually the clouds cleared. Seeds from some plants and the roots of others had survived, and they began to grow again. Life went on.

But the kings were dead. After ruling for 135 million years, the dinosaurs were gone, and the world was free for the taking.

Lizard

24

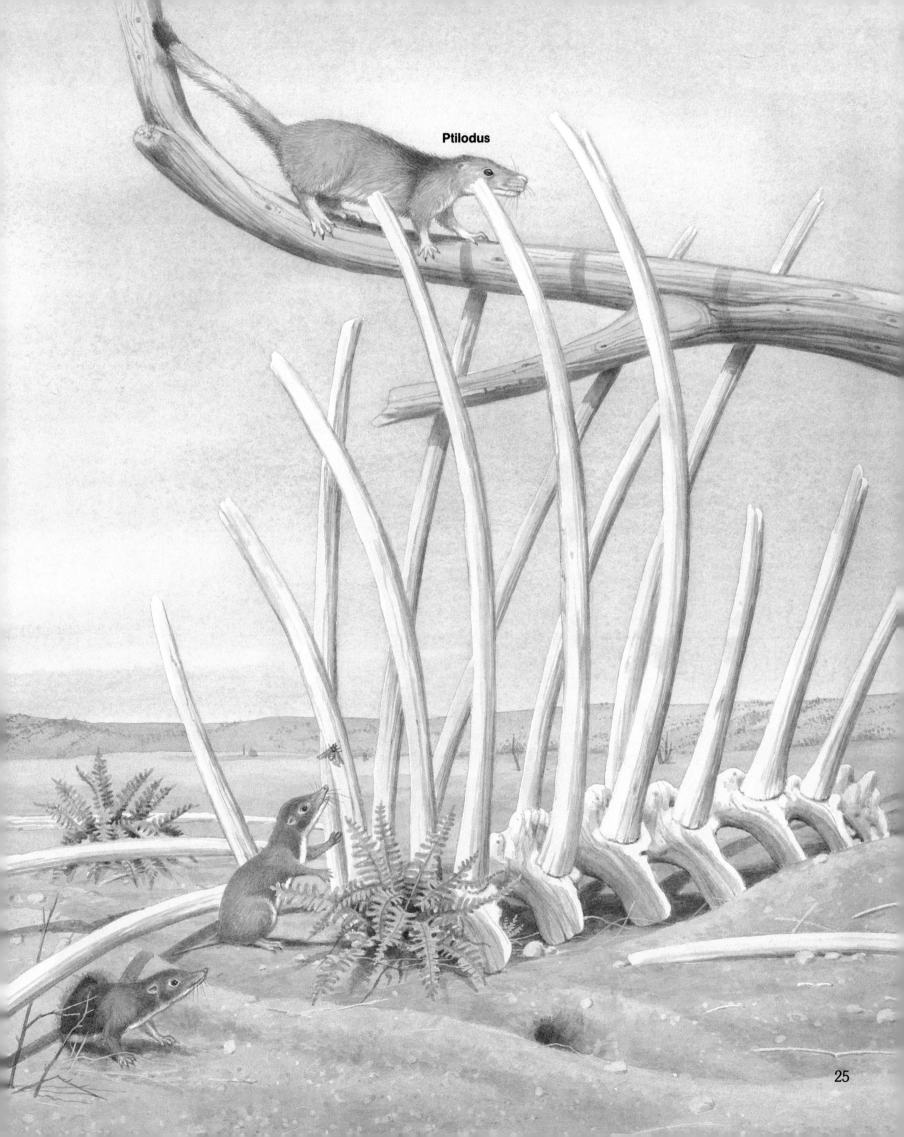

Ptilodus

The Last Challenger

Without dinosaurs the world was virtually empty and much safer for mammals. Not all danger died with the dinosaurs, though.

A new monster, **Diatryma** the "terror bird," took the place of the vanished killer dinosaurs. It could not fly, but its powerful legs helped it run down its victims.

For nearly 20 million years Diatryma was the most dangerous flesh-eater on Earth. Peaceful plant-eating mammals like **Meniscotherium** could only run and hide—they were helpless against Diatryma. No mammal alive then was a match for it.

Birds are descended from dinosaurs. In a way it was fitting that a monstrous bird would be first to try to take over from its ancestors.

Diatryma and other birds never became as dominant as the dinosaurs, though, and eventually the 10-foot-tall bird of prey disappeared.

Meanwhile the lowly mammals were at last beginning to grow more powerful.

Diatryma

Meniscotherium

27

Barylambda

Pantolambda

The Age of the Mammals

For several million years after the dinosaurs were gone, mammals continued to scurry in and out of their burrows. They kept to the underbrush, shadows, and trees, just as if they expected the dinosaurs to reappear at any moment.

Finally a few bold mammals began to enter some of the environments left empty by the dead dinosaurs. In time two new types of mammals evolved. One, called **Pantolambda**, was as big as a large sheep. It was a plant-eater that spent much of its time in the water. The other was **Barylambda**, a heavy, thick-legged eight-foot-long creature that ate leaves from shrubs and trees.

As strange-looking and unimpressive as these two were, their existence showed that mammals were coming out of their holes to lay claim to the world.

29

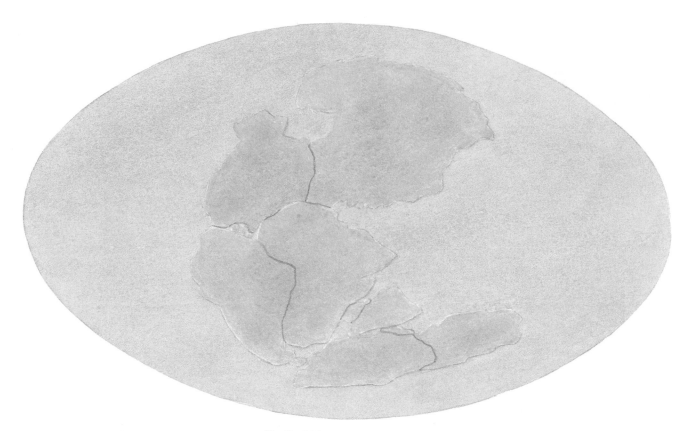

Earth, 230 million years ago

But the world had changed since the beginning of the dinosaurs' rule. Then, all the land on Earth had been fused into a single, huge continent called **Pangea**. By the time the dinosaurs were dead, Pangea had broken into pieces, which very slowly moved apart. This movement of continents is called **continental drift**.

One big piece of Pangea was **Africa**. Another was **South America**. Another one included both **Australia** and **Antarctica**, still fused together. The last one included **North America** and **Eurasia**, which were also still fused. Oceans filled the spaces between the new continents.

Early mammals had spread throughout Pangea before it broke up, so there were some of them on each of the pieces. By the time the dinosaurs were dead, the wide oceans between the new continents were all but impossible for the mammals to cross. The mammals were trapped where they were.

So when the mammals came out of the shadows, they found a divided world awaiting them. On different continents, in different environments, separate groups of mammals evolved in different ways to become the new, true kings of the world. How these new kings would fare in the ever-changing world was yet to be seen. Still, the mammals' age of glory had arrived.

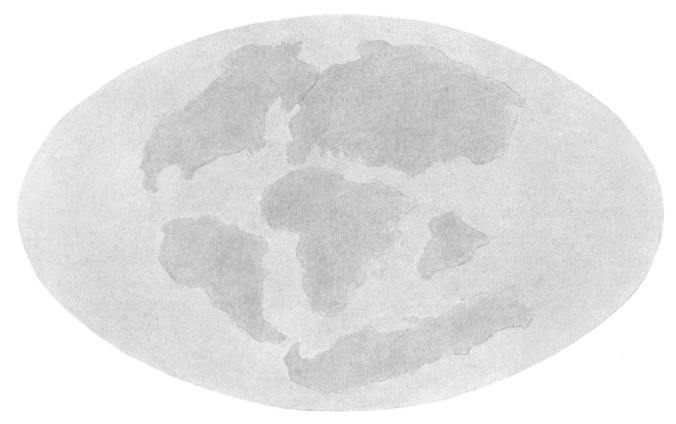

Earth, 60 million years ago

Earth, today

The Ugly American

North America and Eurasia were well stocked with primitive mammals from which new kinds of animals might evolve. Around 50 million years ago an amazing surge of evolutionary development began to take place in North America.

Many of the mammals that evolved were early forerunners of animals that are well known today. One of these was **Hyracotherium**, the first member of the horse family. Hyracotherium was a forest creature that fed on the leaves of plants growing on the forest floor. It evolved from a type of primitive mammal called a **condylarth**.

At about the same time, early forms of rhinoceroses were also evolving from different condylarths. Later, from still other condylarths, the first pigs, camels, and cowlike creatures evolved. At first, though, all of these were piggish-looking creatures.

Patriofelis

Toward the end of the North American surge of evolution, the earliest forms of goats, sheep, antelope, deer, llamas, giraffes, and hippopotamuses also made their appearance, thanks again to those very capable condylarths.

Though they weren't the direct ancestors of modern dogs and cats, meat-eating doglike and catlike creatures also existed in those days. **Dromocyon** was a fierce doglike animal that hunted in packs. **Patriofelis**, a huge, powerful catlike killer, was the greatest terror of the time.

The ugliest creature of its time, and maybe the ugliest mammal of all time, was a powerful, giant plant-eater called **Uintatherium**. Armed with six knobby horns and two long saber-tooth fangs for self-defense, it was probably as safe from meat-eaters as it was from winning beauty contests.

Uintatherium

Lords of Thunder

The dusty plain shook under their feet as two **Brontotherium** bulls battled over a mate. Though bloodied and tired, the younger bull lunged again, ramming its massive Y-shaped horn into its rival's side with all the strength its five tons of muscle could muster. There was a loud crack. The older bull staggered away, two of its ribs broken. In time, the ribs would heal, but the older bull's days as the leader of the herd were over.

Not far away from the scene of this dramatic struggle a huge, heavy **Moropus** peacefully munched leaves.

Moropus and Brontotherium both thrived but in different ways. Strange-looking Moropus, with its catlike feet and horselike head, ate leaves from tree branches that it pulled into reach using its front claws. Its unusual eating habits set it apart from other animals.

Brontotherium

34

Moropus

Brontotherium was less original in how it filled its belly, grazing in an ordinary way. It shared its source of food with other animals. But Brontotherium was well suited to the environment and became very abundant. It may have eaten up more and more of the same food supply that Uintatherium depended upon. In time, Uintatherium died out. Brontotherium, which means "thunder beast," eventually dominated the flatlands of North America and became the new lord of the land.

Giants of Eurasia

Two giants walked the Asian soil. One was the largest meat-eating land mammal that ever lived. The other, a plant-eater, was the largest land mammal of all time.

The meat-eater was called **Andrewsarchus**. It looked somewhat like a dog—but a dog that came right out of a nightmare! Andrewsarchus had long sharp teeth and a huge powerful body. Its head alone was 3 feet long, and its whole body may have been over 12 feet long. Possibly Andrewsarchus hunted in packs, like dogs, making it even more dangerous. But sometimes big meat-eaters don't form packs, so it's also possible that Andrewsarchus hunted alone, like a bear.

Andrewsarchus wasn't really related to dogs or bears. It was a **creodont**, one of the first flesh-eating mammals. Andrewsarchus must have been the most feared creature of the Asian foothills.

36

Andrewsarchus

Indricotherium

There was one mammal of Eurasia, however, that probably feared nothing. This was **Indricotherium**, the biggest of all giant mammals.

Indricotherium was usually quiet, except when it moved its 20-ton body to the next tree to reach a fresh supply of leaves. Each footstep must have sounded like a giant drumbeat.

Indricotherium was an early form of rhinoceros, though it had no thick armor or horns. Then again, such a big mammal wouldn't need extra protection. Its size and strength alone probably would have discouraged any meat-eater—even Andrewsarchus.

No one knows how long Indricotherium lived, but while it did, it surely was the king of beasts in Eurasia.

Back to the Sea

Africa was already home to many primitive mammals by the time continental drift separated it from other lands. Some of its mammals evolved in ways similar to their relatives elsewhere. But since conditions were different in Africa, some creatures evolved in strange and fantastic ways.

Very early on in its history as a separate land, doglike hunters called **mesonychids** slowly began to move into Africa's large, swampy forests. It is possible that their mongooselike competitors, **hyaenodonts**, crowded them out of their usual homes.

Basilosaurus family

Over millions of years some mesonychids evolved until they were at home in the water. Eventually some of them became more and more suited to living their lives completely in the water.

Finally, after many, many evolutionary steps, descendants of the mesonychids became the first whales. One of their kind, the mighty **Basilosaurus**, was the terror of the seas 50 million years ago.

Everywhere else in the world the descendants of the mesonychids slowly died out. But whales descended from the African mesonychids still swim the seas, including the powerful sperm whale and the huge blue whale—the largest animal of any kind in the history of the world.

Arsinoitherium

Africa—A History of Mystery

Forty million years ago a huge plant-eater named **Arsinoitherium** plodded heavily through Africa's forests and splashed across its wooded wetlands. Arsinoitherium may have been the mightiest African mammal of its time. No one knows what its predecessors were like, or if it had any descendants. If it did, they probably weren't around long.

Moeritherium

One neighbor of Arsinoitherium was **Moeritherium**, the earliest member of the elephant family. Moeritherium was a trunkless pig-sized animal that ate juicy reeds growing along the edges of ponds and streams. Probably it often hid in the murky water to avoid meat-eating enemies. What were they like? No one knows for sure.

Little is known about early African mammals. Primitive plant-eating, insect-eating, shrewlike, and ratlike mammals must have lived in Africa from the earliest times. But traces of those first creatures and their earlier descendants are few. Most of the early life history of Africa has yet to be discovered.

When Continents Collide

Two million years ago, under the leafy ceiling of a South American jungle, **Smilodon**, the saber-toothed cat, stalked a creature it had never seen before. But it was hungry and not very picky about victims. The slow-moving **glyptodon** plodded along, showing no concern. With claws bared and fangs ready to stab and slash, the saber-toothed cat leapt onto the glyptodon's back—and promptly bounced right off. Snarling, the big cat scrambled to its feet. Before it could attack again, though, a heavy blow from the glyptodon's powerful armored tail caught it solidly on the shoulder, sending it sprawling again. After deciding there must be easier meals to kill, the cat fled, limping, while the glyptodon simply plodded on.

Armor-plated glyptodon from South America and saber-toothed Smilodon from North America weren't the only new animals who were meeting each other for the first time around two million years ago. Many, many such meetings were happening because a major change had taken place in the world.

Smilodon

Glyptodon

South America had been cut off from other lands for 60 million years. During that time its primitive mammals had evolved into a wide variety of creatures. Many of them were **marsupials**. Marsupials are mammals that carry their babies in pouches for a while after they're born.

The slow process of continental drift finally brought South America very near North America. Volcanoes in the sea between them poured out lava, which cooled into new land, helping to form Central America, which became a bridge connecting them.

Megatherium

Thylacosmilus

Opossum

Glyptode

44

After 60 million years apart, the creatures of North and South America could pass back and forth and mingle.

Many North American and South American mammals looked and acted amazingly alike. But the North American mammals were **placentals**. Placentals are mammals whose babies are born more fully developed than marsupial babies. Placental babies don't need to be carried in a pouch. This gave the North American mammals an advantage. Some of them had other advantages, too. Within a short time most of the South American mammals died out and were replaced by their North American cousins.

So Smilodon eventually did find many an easier meal.

Glyptodon did all right for itself, too. Like the giant sloth **Megatherium**, the **opossum**, and a few other South American mammals, it survived the North American invasion and spread well into North America, where the opossum is alive today.

Macrauchenia

Toxodon

Diprotodon, a giant wombat bigger than a modern rhinoceros—the largest marsupial that ever lived

Echidna

The Last Stronghold

When Australia became isolated from the rest of the world, only very primitive mammals lived there. For 64 million years generation after generation of these creatures have lived on their island continent with very little interference.

Like Africa, Australia offers little evidence about the early evolution of its animals. But there is evidence that some of the creatures there have changed only a little over the countless generations since the day their ancestors arrived.

Many of Australia's mammals are marsupials, like those that once ruled South America. In South America almost all the marsupials died out after competitors from North America invaded. Australia had no such invasion.

Several million years ago many of Australia's marsupial mammals reached gigantic sizes and became primitive kings ruling over their isolated kingdom.

**Procoptodons,
giant kangaroos**

**Thylacoleo,
a lionlike marsupial**

Duckbill platypus

Two creatures currently alive in Australia are **monotremes**. Though they are considered mammals, they lay eggs like reptiles. They are the only two monotremes in the world, the last of their kind.

It is possible that these two Australian monotremes, the **duckbill platypus** and the **echidna**, are actually surviving examples of two of the very earliest mammals, close relatives of the mammal-like reptiles that died out 200 million years ago.

If that is so, Australia is truly the last stronghold of ancient life on Earth.

The Rise of Man

In Africa and in South America, mammals called **primates** evolved from small primitive shrewlike creatures into many varieties of monkeys.

In South America, monkeys remained in the trees, but in Africa, their development did not stop there.

Nearly 30 million years ago the climate in Africa began changing. Forests began to thin out, leaving wide-open grassy plains. Some **apes**, which had evolved from the monkeys, began to live on the plains instead of in the trees.

By 20 million years ago the first manlike apes had evolved.

About six million years ago the earliest ancestors of man, the **australopithecines**, appeared. They continued to develop, showing more and more signs of becoming men. Finally, about two million years ago, some of the australopithecines living in East Africa began to make tools from stones, build simple shelters, and use long bones as weapons.

They were the first humans.

Australopithecus

Homo erectus

50

Out of Africa

About 20 million years ago continental drift carried Africa back into contact with Eurasia. Once the way was open, many African mammals, including members of the elephant family, porcupines, and apes, spread to Europe and Asia, while rhinoceroses, cats, jackals, antelope, and other mammals entered Africa. These animals continued to evolve and adapt in their new homes.

The australopithecines also crossed into Eurasia. By six million years ago the australopithecines were spread far and wide across Africa and Eurasia, continuing to evolve everywhere they went. The new humans who descended from the australopithecines about one and three-quarter million years ago were called **Homo erectus**.

Homo erectus was the first human to discover the use of fire, and eventually he learned to make and control it.

Fire gave Homo erectus light and warmth. It cooked his food. But, eventually, Homo erectus learned that fire was more than that—it was a tool unlike any other.

On an autumn day 250,000 years ago, a band of Homo erectus hid and waited in a narrow valley. It was cold, and though they were huddled together and draped in furry pelts, the men were probably shivering. Finally they saw what they were waiting for—a herd of elephants, migrating south as winter approached. Once the huge beasts had entered their trap, the men started fires in carefully chosen places. The blazes spread through the dry grass and underbrush and roared up into walls of flame. Terrified, the elephants ran in the only direction open to them—right into a soft, muddy bog. There, stuck in the mud, they were easy for the hunters to kill and butcher with their stone axes.

Some say that this was the end of the Age of Mammals and the beginning of the Age of Man.

Neanderthal man

The Ice Age Comes

It started two million years ago. Year by year, the weather grew colder, the snows fell harder, spring came later, and summer ended sooner. In areas near the North and South poles, huge sheets of ice formed. Every year they got larger, spreading across the land until much of the world was covered year-round with ice.

As the ice spread down across Europe, North America, and Asia, mammals and all other animals fled to the south to escape the cold. All except one.

Mankind, because of its new tool—fire—didn't fear the cold.

Woolly mammoths

Woolly rhinoceros

Many humans moved north into new areas, where migrating animals provided easy hunting.

Some mammals—such as woolly mammoths, woolly rhinoceroses, and musk oxen—evolved thick coats of fur as protection against the cold. But man had entered a new stage of evolution. His increasing brain capacity had eliminated the need for very **specific adaptations** like coats of fur. His ability to think was a **general adaptation** that allowed him to solve any problems he faced. No longer was he just another animal, entirely at the mercy of stronger animals and the environment. He was man, the thinker; man, the tool maker; man, the user of fire.

Man, the new ruler of Earth.

Man, the Communicator

Around 200,000 years ago Homo erectus gradually evolved into **Homo sapiens**. Some of these early Homo sapiens were called **Neanderthals**. They were smarter and more capable than Homo erectus. Another type of Homo sapiens, the **Cro-Magnon**, evolved about 40,000 years ago and rapidly became the dominant type of humankind. Cro-Magnon men were the first humans who looked like people do today.

As man evolved so did his ability to speak. Homo erectus probably had a simple language that was not much different from the noise signals some animals use to communicate among themselves. Cro-Magnon men probably had well-developed spoken languages.

At some point, as men learned to speak, they began to ask questions about themselves and their place in the world. But those questions, and the ideas they may have inspired in men's imaginations, are long lost and forgotten.

Cro-Magnon man

Anetoceras

Palaeolimulus

Hypsognathus

Bothriolepis

Seymouria

Erythrosuchus

Tyrannosaurus rex

Diplodocus

Stegosaurus

Dimetrodon

Diatryma

Uintatherium

Hyaenodon

Thylacosmilus

Brontotherium

Macrauchenia

56

During the last 40,000 years most of the few remaining giants of the Age of Mammals have died out. The great ice sheets have melted away, at least for a while, and mankind has learned to farm, to tame animals, and to build cities. Man has invented both terrible and wonderful things. But perhaps the greatest of man's inventions started 30,000 years ago, when Cro-Magnon men painted the stories of their hunts on the walls of caves. This was the simple beginning of writing—a great leap in man's ability to communicate.

As written language developed, man, the questioner, man, the imaginer, at last had the means to preserve his thoughts and ideas, as well as the questions that inspired them.

As the ruler of Earth, man is different from all the kings that went before. No others knew they were kings. None of them could spread knowledge or pass it down to their children. None of them had history.

Man, the communicator, can share what he has learned with those around him and with his descendants as well. Generations yet to come will inherit not only our world, but our knowledge. Building upon the foundation of the thoughts and ideas handed down to him, perhaps man of the future will find answers to the questions he faces.

Baluchitherium

Woolly mammoth

Synthetoceras

Megatherium

Horse

Dryopithecus

Australopithecus

Man

GLOSSARY/ PRONUNCIATION GUIDE

Allosaurus (al-lo-SAW-rus)
A giant meat-eating dinosaur that lived about 160 million years ago

amphibians (am-FIB-ee-ans)
Egg-laying animals that live part of their lives in water and part on land

Andrewsarchus (an-droo-SAR-kus)
The largest meat-eating land mammal, probably 12 feet long. Andrewsarchus lived in Asia over 40 million years ago.

Arsinoitherium (ar-sin-oy-THEER-ee-um)
A giant four-horned plant-eating mammal that lived in Africa 40 million years ago

australopithecines (aw-stray-lo-PITH-uh-seens)
The first humans. Australopithecines evolved around six million years ago in Africa.

Basilosaurus (ba-sih-lo-SAW-rus)
A meat-eating whale that lived 45 million years ago

Brontotherium (bron-tow-THEER-ee-um)
A large plant-eating mammal that roamed North American plains 35 million years ago. Brontotherium means "thunder beast."

ceratopsians (ser-uh-TOP-see-ans)
Plant-eating horned dinosaurs

comet
A mass of ice, dust, and rocks that orbits the sun. The sun's radiation makes comets appear to be fiery, with long glowing tails.

condylarths (KON-dee-larths)
Prehistoric mammals from which the first ancestors of modern cows, camels, giraffes, pigs, llamas, and other mammals evolved

continental drift
The slow movement of Earth's land masses

cotylosaurs (KO-tuhl-o-sawrs)
Prehistoric reptiles from which dinosaurs, birds, and modern reptiles evolved

creodont (KREE-uh-dahnt)
A type of prehistoric meat-eating mammal. Andrewsarchus was a creodont.

Cro-Magnon (krow-MAN-yon)
A type of Homo sapiens that evolved around 40,000 years ago. Cro-Magnon looked like modern man.

Diatryma (die-uh-TRY-ma)
The "terror bird." Diatryma was a 10-foot-tall meat-eating bird that lived 60 million years ago.

Dimetrodon (die-MEH-truh-don)
A 12-foot-long meat-eating pelycosaur that was the terror of its time, 270 million years ago

dinosaurs (DIE-no-sawrs)
Powerful relatives of the reptiles that ruled Earth from 200 million years ago until 65 million years ago

Dromocyon (drow-MO-see-on)
A fierce doglike hunter that roamed in packs across North America 50 million years ago

duckbill platypus (DUHK-bill PLAD-uh-pus)
One of the last two monotremes in the world. Like the other surviving monotreme, the echidna, it lives in Australia.

echidna (uh-KID-nuh)
One of the last two monotremes in the world. Like its relative the duckbill platypus, it lays eggs.

environment
All of the external conditions and factors that affect a living thing

evolution
The process by which living things change from generation to generation

fossils
Remains or traces of ancient life; usually the remains of bones

glyptodon (GLIP-tuh-don)
A large armor-plated mammal that evolved in South America and spread into North America. It died out only a million years ago.

hadrosaurs (HAD-row-sawrs)
Plant-eating duck-billed dinosaurs

Homo erectus (HOE-mo ee-RECK-tuhs)
A type of early man that evolved around one and three quarter million years ago. Homo erectus was the first kind of human to use fire.

Homo sapiens (HOE-mo SAY-pee-enz)
A type of human being that evolved 200,000 years ago. Modern humans are homo sapiens.

hyaenodonts (hie-EE-nuh-dahnts)
Early flesh-eating mammals. They were mongooselike animals, though modern mongooses are not descended from hyaenodonts.

Hyracotherium (hie-rack-o-THEER-ee-um)
The earliest ancestor of the modern horse

Ichthyostega (ick-thee-o-STAY-guh)
The first amphibian

Indricotherium (in-dree-ko-THEER-ee-um)
The largest land mammal ever. Indricotherium was a plant-eater that lived in Asia about 40 million years ago.

mammals
Animals that are warm-blooded, have fur or hair, give birth to live babies instead of laying eggs, and nurse their young

marsupials (mar-SOO-pee-uhls)
Mammals that carry their young in pouches for some time after they are born

Megatherium (meg-uh-THEER-ee-um)
A giant ground sloth that evolved in South America and spread into North America. It probably died out within the last thousand years.

Meniscotherium (men-iss-ko-THEER-ee-um)
A type of condylarth that lived 65 million years ago

mesonychids (meh-ZON-ih-kids)
Early meat-eating doglike mammals from which whales evolved

Moeritherium (meer-uh-THEER-ee-um)
The earliest ancestor of the modern elephant

monotremes (MAH-no-treems)
Mammals that lay eggs. Monotremes are closely related to the very earliest mammals that evolved 200 million years ago.

Morganucodon (more-gan-OO-kuh-don)
The first mammal. Morganucodon evolved around 200 million years ago.

Moropus (MORE-uh-pus)
A large North American plant-eating mammal with a horselike head and catlike feet

Neanderthals (nee-AN-duh-thols)
Early Homo sapiens

Pangea (pan-JEE-uh)
The single huge continent that existed more than 230 million years ago. All the land in the world was part of Pangea.

Patriofelis (pa-tree-o-FEE-luhs)
An early catlike meat-eating mammal

pelycosaurs (PELL-uh-ko-sawrs)
The earliest forerunners of mammals. These mammal-like reptiles dominated the world from 280 million years ago until 200 million years ago.

prehistoric
Before recorded history

primates
Mammals that include monkeys, apes, and man

reptiles
Animals that are cold-blooded and lay their eggs on land, as opposed to in water like amphibians

Smilodon (SMY-luh-don)
A large saber-toothed cat that evolved in North America and spread into South America, Europe, and Asia

thecodonts (THEE-kuh-dahnts)
The immediate forerunners of the dinosaurs

theories
Guesses made on the basis of evidence

therapsids (thuh-RAP-suhds)
The immediate forerunners of mammals

Tyrannosaurus rex (tuh-ran-uh-SAW-rus rex)
A huge, powerful meat-eating dinosaur. Its name means "tyrant lizard king."

Uintatherium (oo-in-tuh-THEER-ee-um)
A large North American plant-eating mammal that evolved around 50 million years ago and still holds the record for ugliness

INDEX